The War

Yo-Yo

Kid

ANNELÉ JEANETTE SHAW

Order this book online at www.trafford.com
or email orders@trafford.com

Most Trafford titles are also available at major online book retailers.

Printed in the United States of America.

ISBN: 978-1-4907-0785-3 (sc)
ISBN: 978-1-4907-0784-6 (e)

Trafford rev. 09/16/2013

   www.trafford.com

North America & international
toll-free: 1 888 232 4444 (USA & Canada)
fax: 812 355 4082

CONTENTS

INTRODUCTION 1

THE WAR YO-YO KID 6

THE THREE (3) WARS 8

MY FATHER...15

1939-1941 20

MY MOM 23

MY SIBLINGS MAJ 26

SVEN...29

SYLVIA...32

LEA..35

MY BROTHER LEO 38

EILA 47

GUNNEL...52

ARRIVING IN DENMARK 54

MY DANISH FAMILY 62

MY DANISH FAMILY. (MOR) 68

ARNE 73

BENTE 78

AGE FOUR 82

THE GERMAN OCCUPATION OF DENMARK 84

SONJA..86

THE TRIP TO THE COUNTRYSIDE.........................90

STARTING SCHOOL 94

THE GARDEN...100

LEAVING DENMARK.......................................103

BACK IN FINLAND...108

DANISH CITIZEN 112

MENTOR..114

MY CONFIRMATION.......................................115

MY LIFE IN NYKOBING FALSTER........................119

BORNI...124

MOVING BACK TO HASLEV 133

HASLEV 139

A VISIT TO JENSEN'S SHOP 141

VACATIONS..147

CHRISTMAS IN DENMARK................................158

HUSASSISTENTERNES FAGSKOLE 164

LONDON 168

LILO 175

PARIS 178

THE INVITATION TO USA 185

THE ARRIVAL IN NEW YORK.............................190

THE SCANDINAVIAN TRIP IN 2011 195

THE CHALLENGE..200

INTRODUCTION

Many times during my adult life I have been told by friends and acquaintances, who already knew bits and pieces about my rather unusual and confusing childhood and my life in general, that I should definitely write a biography or book about my life and upbringing, It has made me think about it and I finally decided that it probably would be a good idea.

It has taken me a long time to finish this book, because nobody in my present surroundings is able to help me with this project.

An old professor once told me: "When you write this book, make sure you map it".

That is exactly what I have been trying to do in order to get it in the right sequence of events. It has not been an easy task, since I am now writing this many years later.

I might remember something that happened about fifty five years ago and maybe think of something which took place five, eight or ten years earlier.

I don't consider myself much of a writer at all, but hope that it might turn out to be an interesting story anyway. Some people have even suggested that it could make a very good movie as well. Over the years, when some things from different times in my life have been brought to my mind, I started to write it down. Therefore it has taken a long time to get this book put together.

There have been many long passages of time between the different articles and happenings; At times I would write it in Danish or Swedish and other times in English. There have also been certain episodes and memories which were too unpleasant and hurtful, to write down. I would much rather block it out of my mind.

"What are you going to name "The Book", people would ask me.

The first title that came to my mind was, "Why doesn't anybody want me?", as that was how I often felt as a young and lost child, I was sent around from one family and country to another, starting at age 1 1/2 or 18 months, and it wasn't just to somebody in the neighborhood, but to completely foreign people in a different country with different customs and different languages I didn't understand.

It was a very uncertain and scary experience for a young child.

Later on I learned, of course, that it was for protection during the war situation. Both the parents and the government wanted to save the children from all the bombing and destruction that was taking place in the war torn Finland at that time.

Many families were separated and their lives were shattered.

One Mother said: "It is better to have your child 100 miles away and safe, instead of having him or her in a grave next to you".

I have to add that I am very blessed and fortunate that several years later I got to meet and know my birth family again.

I chose another name for the book: "THE WAR YO-YO KID".

LEA WITH ME IN THE STROLER

ANNELE

SVEN

FINLAND

FINLAND (The red blobs are the Russian army,
the blue ones are the Finish defence troups)

THE WAR YO-YO KID

I was born in Helsinki, Finland on a very cold Sunday morning, January 30, 1938, and I was given the name Annele Jeanette Selander. I was baptized or christened in Kallio Lutheran Church on March 31, 1938.

(My sisters told me later, that they picked the middle name Jeanette after the movie actress JEANETTE McDONALD).

It was one of the coldest winters the Scandinavian Countries had experienced in several years, at least so I was told.

The Country was totally cowered with mountains of powdery white snow and the traffic in the City of Helsinki had almost come to a stand still.

Anybody, who braved the freezing cold temperatures and dared to venture out doors, was dressed like Eskimos and only did so out of necessity, or to go to work.

My family was at that time living in an apartment building in Snellmansgatan in Helsinki. I have since visited Snellmansgatan to try to find the building, but it no longer exists. Whether it was bombed during the war or just torn down, I don't know.

I was the youngest girl out of a family of eight (8) siblings, six (6) girls and two (2) boys.

Only about one year after I was born, the Russian-Finish War started, when Russia attacked Finland during the winter of 1939. It turned out to be three individual wars, which lasted to 25 April, 1945.

SNELLMANSGATAN

SNELLMAN IN FRONT OF THE FINISH BANK

THE THREE (3) WARS

M ost people have never heard of the 3 wars.

First "THE WINTER WAR" 1939-1940.
"THE CONTINUATION WAR" 1941-1944.
"THE THIRD WAR" 1944-1945.

In the fall of 1939 the European countries & Russia had a lot of disagreements.

(The disagreements were primarily over political & geographical problems).

Russia (Soviet Union) was dissatisfied over the fact that St. Petersburg, which at that time was Leningrad, didn't have free exit out to open waters, but was somewhat isolated. They wanted to take the Karelian area and the eastern part of Finland as well as the peninsula in the northeast out to "Ishavet".

Finland of course did not want to give up part of the country, so Russia attacked the much smaller country— Finland.

Finland had about 21,600 soldiers and Russia had 120.000 soldiers.

Naturally Russia was much too overpowering, so they ended up, in spite of much opposition from the Fins, taking Karelen and big parts of the eastern border of Finland as well as "The Arm" in the north. Finland was totally unprepared for war, "THE WINTER WAR" only lasted a little over 3 months (100 days).

Stalin thought Russia was going to take over Finland in a couple of weeks and estimated that the Russian Army would be arriving in Helsinki in that short time, but he found out that it was not that simple. The fact is that they never got there. They did take the Karelian area with the town Viipuri, (Viborg). Many Finish families were able to escape that area, as they did not want to be under Russian Government.

Petsamo, the town in the northern most part of Finland, was also lost.

While this "WINTER WAR" was taking place, Finland had started to send a lot of their youngest children out of the country to protect them. That was the time I along with 3 other sisters and 1 brother were sent to Sweden to completely unknown people. We came to different families in the northern part of Sweden. I was the youngest sibling in our family and at that time I was only 18 months old. Quite frankly, I didn't understand what was happening.

Since "THE WINTER WAR" only lasted few months we were all sent back home to our families in Finland again in April-May, 1940.

Finland had to agree on a "Truce" with Russia in March, 1940.

In June, 1941 Germany (Hitler's Weld) started to attack Russia (Operation Barbarossa). This was now called "THE CONTINUATION WAR". As the peace period didn't last very long and Finland was still hoping to win back all the parts of the country they had lost to Russia. Germany and Finland were now allies against Russia. However, in many areas they disagreed on things. Hitler wanted Finland to attack Leningrad (St. Petersburg), which Finland refused to do as well as deport all the Jews and send them to Concentration Camps in Germany. Finland wanted no part in that.

By now Finland was fighting both Russia and Germany, "THE CONTINUATION WAR" had now started. Once again the Finish Government saw no other way of saving their children than to send them out of the country for protection.

About (Sixty-five thousand) 65000 children were shipped out of the country this time. Most of them were sent to Sweden, about (Four thousand) 4000 were sent on to Denmark and a few to Norway.

In December 1941, as the youngest and only one from my family, I was sent away again. My sisters and brothers were school age and my oldest brother was old enough to be recruited into the military, so they were staying in Finland this time.

I was now 3 years old and spoke both Finish & Swedish. This time I was not sent to Sweden but to Denmark.

Together with several hundred kids, I was transported by train from Helsinki to Turku (Aabo) where we boarded a ship to Stockholm, Sweden. Some of us were placed in schools and others in hospitals for lodging for 1 or 2 nights, We were fed sandwiches, milk and fruit, If any of the children were sick or had colds they were attended by doctors before they were sent on to the different destinations.

At first there were talks about sending the children to special centers for the duration of the war. But most people disagreed with that idea.

I was again placed on board a train together with a lot of other kids and nurses on our way to our unknown destinations, heading south through Sweden towards Denmark. When we arrived in Copenhagen we were once again checked by a medical staff to assure that we were healthy and not bringing any contagious diseases to our new surroundings.

Because of many private arrangements the exact number of children who were shipped out of Finland is a bit unknown. The number of children arriving in Denmark was estimated at 4000. The building holding the archives in Copenhagen, containing the names and ages of the Finish children, were burned to the ground so the Germans couldn't get that information.

"THE THIRD WAR" was started in 1944 as Russia wanted to throw all the German troops out of Finland, as they were now fighting Russia on Finnish soil. That made that war even more devastating for people still living in Finland, especially the one's living close to the border, eastern parts of the country, and Lapland. Further more, when the German troupes were forced to leave Finland, they completely destroyed and burned large areas of Lapland and eastern parts of Finland closest to the Russian border as revenge towards Russia & Finland.

The town Rovaniemi in the northern part of Finland was totally destroyed. Every house was burned to the ground before the German Army left the Country.

The war in Finland lasted to 25 April, 1945.

After the war was ended, Russia demanded that Finland pay Russia a large war death. Finland was forced to send most of their productions to Russia for many years. Finland was also the first Country to pay off all their war deaths to USA.

MY PARENTS

FINISH SKI TROUPS

PRESIDENT MANAHEIM

MY FATHER

My Dad, Matti Selander was born September 25, 1890 in a small town, Kuhmainen in the central part of Finland.

Unfortunately I have very little information and knowledge about my Dad's childhood, family and ancestry. I do know that he only had one sister, who was older than he and whom I never met.

The main reason for the lack of information about my Dad as well as the rest of the family is primarily because I was separated and away from the family most of the time, but from the little time I was able to spend together with him I know that he was an excellent carpenter and made some great wood works. One of the things he made was a wooden rocking horse he made for me and my sisters. He also made an intricate looking dumbwaiter, which my parents had staying in their house for many years.

My Dad built a two story mountain/summer house by himself in the country side, Jupper, not too far from Helsinki. That is where the whole Selander family spent most of their time, when they were not working or the kids didn't have to attend school.

The house was built on a big piece of land, of about four acres, that my Father had purchased several years earlier and he built the house in between his regular jobs. It was a beautiful 2 story house and since the family was large the house had to be big enough to house everybody at one time.

I loved being there in the summer time, especially playing or working with my Mom in the garden planting flowers, vegetables, fruit or other things. We had many animals, several cats, a dog, a goat, a horse and lots of rabbits in cages.

Later on my Dad built a smaller house close to the main house, where my Grandmother, (my Mother's Mom) lived for several years, so they could take care of her in her old age.

Unfortunately my time enjoying my life in the country side and in Finland in general was very limited.

My Father was in the Finish Army during the Finish-Russian War and was shot & wounded in one of his legs. He still had a lot of problems with the leg many years later.

ISA DAD   AITI

THE HOUSE MY MOM GREW UP IN

THE SELANDER FAMILY

ANTON VISITING THE SELANDER FAMILY

GUNNEL, ME, ANTON, AITI (MOM)

5 SIBLINGS
Lea, Me, Sven, Gunnel, Sylvia

MAJ'S HOUSE

MOM AND EILA

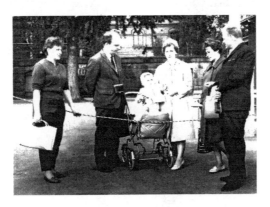

1939-1941

U nfortunately I don't remember hardly anything about what was happening during the time I was back home in Finland, after I had been in Sweden for a few months at age 1 ½-3. I was sent away again in 1941, when I was 3 years old. I guess I was too young to remember any ordinary things, but I do remember times when there were a lot of noise. It was probably when the war had started again and we were under bomb attacks by Russia.

Everybody was very nervous and upset and we had to hurry up and run down to the basement, where it was very dark and cold. That was the only place you could hide and feel a little safer. Obviously that scared me too and must have made a big impression on me, because I many times afterwards suffered from having bad nightmares about being attacked.

Maj, Nils & me.

MAJ AND ME AT OUR
PARENT'S GRAVE

Annele, Kenneth and Maj

AITI

MY MOM

My Mom, "Äiti" (Finish for Mother), Augusta Mathilde Westerberg was born and grew up in the south western part of Finland on a small island called Hitis. She was born January 9, 1895.

The people living in that part of the country primarily speak Swedish with Finish as a secondary language.

After finishing high school she decided to move to Helsinki, hoping to find a job in the city. She got her first job in a small office doing filing etc. That was not very interesting to her. She decided she would like to do some traveling, so she managed to get a job on one of the cruise ships sailing between Finland, Sweden and Great Britain. At first she worked as a waitress and server, even though she had no experience as such.

She liked to cook, so she started working in the kitchen on board the ship. Pretty soon they found out that she was very artistic and good at making fancy "open face sandwiches" so she was promoted to "Smorrebrods jomfru". Augusta was able to expand her artistic talent. She was now making very colorful, mouthwatering and exciting "open face sandwiches", and other interesting eatables.

She worked on board a couple of different cruise ships for about 3 years when she decided to go back to the city of Helsinki and stay there.

She had a few different jobs, when she was asked by a friend to help with a landscaping job. Some things she had always loved were flowers, plants and animals. That appealed to her very much. Besides, she could be out in the beautiful nature as well as choosing her own hours.

During this time she met a very handsome young man, Matti Selander, whom she later married and who also became the Father of 8 children, 6 girls and 2 boys of which I was the youngest.

Maj

Her Mercedes

Maj's House.

MY SIBLINGS
MAJ

My oldest sister Maj Lempi Maria was born December, 1919. She was for several years staying with an uncle and aunt who did not have any children of their own. They more or less adopted her. She loved living with them as they were able to "spoil" her and give her more attention and certain toys and things that our own parents couldn't give her as they were rather poor at that time.

I was told that Maj was an exceptionally good student. She was very intelligent and was able to speak several different languages at a very young age.

At age 21, she met and married a very successful young man, Nils Krook. He was an engineer and had a great and high ranking job at NOKIA, which at that time were mostly manufacturing tires and other rubberized materials. NOKIA is still to this day one of the leading companies in Europe. The company is primarily known as a mobile/cell phone company.

Nils was a fortunate heir to a large island, which is situated several miles off the west coast of Finland, closest to the city Vaasa. The island is a wonderful vacation spot.

Nils had a house built in Helsinki, which, during the cold winter time, was moved to Vaasa and then pulled across the ice to the island and placed there. Maj, Nils and their two sons, Ray and Kenneth spent a lot of their vacation time enjoying their beautiful island, "Jarvo".

I have also had the opportunity to vacation on the island a few times. When their two boys were school age, they were enrolled in an English Speaking School, which was run by Catholic Nuns in Helsinki. Therefore the boys also spoke several languages at a young age.

Maj & Nils had over the years acquired several houses, apartment buildings, boats and cars. One of their cars was a 1937 Mercedes Benz, which they bought from one of Hitler's Field Marshals, who was stationed in Finland during the war.

When their youngest son, Kenneth, the last one of the Krook family, suddenly had a very untimely death at age fourty (40), a friend of his, mysteriously managed to seize the whole Krook Estate and all of their belongings. That was a very unfortunate happening, as the rest of the family, especially our sisters should have been able to benefit from that Estate.

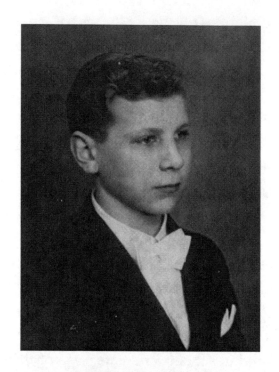

SYLVIA, ANNELE, MAJ,. SVEN, LEA, GUNNEL

SVEN

When the Finish Russian War started in 1939. my oldest brother, Sven, was recruited in to the Finish Army. Sven was only 18 years old at that time and barely finished with the school.

He was very athletic and enjoyed different sports, especially skiing.

When the CONTINUATION WAR started again he was put in charge of one of the ski patrols. When they were fighting the Russian Army they managed to kill and hold back the much larger Russian troops. The Finish Ski troupes were very well trained.

He was however shot through his left hand as well as his stomach and therefore ended up spending a long time in the hospital. He recovered well from his injuries even though it took a long time.

Sven married a Finish girl, Kyliki. They both liked children a lot, but never had any of their own.

After the war he got a job as a security guard at a famous restaurant, which was situated on an island in the

Helsinki harbor area and later as the senior custodian of the parliament building in Helsinki. He even had his own apartment in the building.

Sven was a very likable and funny guy. He had a great sense of humor and managed to keep our Mother and the rest of the family laughing even during the difficult times.

I remember when I was about 5 or 6 years old I liked him so much that I had decided that I was going to marry him . . . . even though I knew he was my own brother.

Since the German Army had also been fighting Russia during the war on Finish soil, Germany and Finland were considered allied. Sven was later awarded a German military Award for heroism, "The Iron Cross", which was signed by Adolph Hitler.

RAINO AND SYLVIA

FOUR SISTERS

EIVOR, TUTA, SYLVIA, TONY, KATI, LEA, ANNELE

SYLVIA

My 3rd. oldest sibling was Sylvia. She was probably the nicest of all eight of us. She was always ready to help any body who needed help. She was a "take charge" kind of person and very good-hearted.

Sylvia was born in Helsinki, like most of us, on August, 1925.

Since she was a lot older than me, she was often put in charge of taking care of me as the youngest one of the children, especially since our Mother was working most of the time or busy with other projects.

She liked to sew and knit. Therefore, she often got the job of sewing and fixing the clothes for us younger kids.

The whole family was very found of animals, especially dogs and cats, and Sylvia was usually the one who would bring home most of the pets that the family owned during the years.

For many years she had a very good and reliable job as an Office Manager for a well known company in Helsinki.

She was married to Raimo Holmstrom, who was a fun loving person. I always used to think of him as a very "Happy-go-lucky" guy.

Sylvia and Raimo had two daughters, Annele and Lisa, but you never heard them being called by their given names. It was always "Pojo" and "Tuta". Tuta still lives in Helsinki, Finland, and Pojo lives in Hamburg, Germany. Unfortunately Sylvia became very ill in 2010-2011. She developed a devastating illness, cancer, and passed away in June, 2011.

TUTA, SEPPO, NIKKE AND KIMMI

LEA, JEANETTE AND BROR   ME AND LEA

EIVOR'S SUMMER HOUSE

LEA

The fourth oldest sibling in the Selander family was Lea. She was born October 8, 1926, just a year after Sylvia, so they were very close to each other when they were very young and they were spending a lot of time together.

One of her first jobs, when she was a teenager, was being an Elevator Operator at the big Stockmann Department store in central Helsinki. She also worked in the music department in the same store selling music sheets etc. That was where she met a young man, Bror Lindfors, who she later married.

In 1966 she started working at the Parliament Building as a Hostess, setting up the different meeting rooms for the dignitaries and public servants, when they had meetings there. She also took care of the sauna rooms in the building. I think she heard a lot of interesting conversation going on in those jobs.

Bror, Lea's husband had his own Electronic Business and store, which he opened up after having worked for Blaupunkt for several years.

Many years in a row they would take a whole month vacation, either in the spring or fall, and rent a condo in Costa Del Sol, Spain.

They had three children, a daughter, Eivor and two sons, Dennis and Bengt. Eivor and Dennis still live in Finland and Bengt, who married a Swedish/American girl, Linda, moved to New Jersey, USA, where they still live.

LEO AND SVEN

LEO VISITING IN HELSINKI

MY VISIT WITH LEO AND FAMILY

MY BROTHER LEO

L eo was number 5 of the 8 siblings in my family. He also ended up in the USA like I did. The life story of his life would make a very interesting book in itself. He definitely had the travel lust just as much or maybe even more than I. He was born in 1929 and he was sent to Sweden together with Lea, Eila, Gunnel and I when the war first broke out between Finland and Russia in 1939.

On that trip he was put in charge of taking care of his four younger sisters. He was only ten (10) years old himself.

At age 14 he had decided to do some traveling of his own, especially since school was not very important to him. He went down to the harbor and managed to get hired on to a Finish fishing boat by lying about his age. He told them that he was 16 years old.

When the boat he was working on was situated somewhere off the Norwegian coast it was captured by the German Navy.

The crew was given a choice to either join the German military or go to German prison camp in Germany. The whole crew chose to go to prison camp, where they were taken to work as forced labor in one of the holocaust camps. I am not sure how long Leo and the crew was kept there.

Needless to say our parents were very worried about what had happened to Leo, as they had no way of finding out where he was.

When he finally got out of prison, he and his friend had to walk and hike their way through Poland and Russia back to Finland.

At times they had to steal and kill chickens, geese and other animals in order to survive. Sometimes they were able to cook the raw meat on a bon fire. Other times they had to eat it uncooked. They managed to find some fruit and vegetables and even dug up potatoes and carrots, wherever they could find some. A few times they were helped by people along the way, but not very often. Their transportation was very sparse, so they stole bikes and blankets wherever they could find some. The trip took place during the winter time, so whenever they found a barn or shack along the way they would spend the nights there. It was a very long exhausting trek.

I remember him telling me that when they got to somewhere in Russia they took the boots he was wearing, so he ended up walking the rest of the way bare foot. When he finally arrived in Helsinki and after a thorough medical check up, the doctors found him to be in fair condition with the exception of being malnourished and exhausted.

Leo stayed in Helsinki and worked for a while before he again wanted to see more of the world. He was particularly interested in seeing Australia. He convinced a friend to join him on his new adventure.

Tom Yering, the son of the Captain of the fishing boat that Leo was on, has also been working on a documentary about his Father's life, the boat and crew as well as the capture of the boat. He did get to talk to Leo on the phone, but unfortunately never got to meet him in person, as Leo passed away in 2009 in Ozark, Alabama, shortly after having triple heart bypass surgery.

When I was in Scandinavia in 2011, I did take a quick trip from Helsingor, Denmark, to Helsingborg, Sweden to meet Tom Yering and his wife. He was at that time still working on the Documentary about his Father's life.

Leo still liked the sea faring life, so he and his "buddy" decided to try to stow away on a freight ship carrying flour. They had to hide in one of the life boats.

They thought the ship was going to Australia, but when the ship was somewhere close to the British coast they thought it was safe to come out from their hiding place, which was close to some pipes in the area where the flour was situated. When they appeared they were covered white with flour and shocked and scared the rest of the crew.

The captain was going to send them back to Finland, when he saw them, but the boys begged him to keep them on board. After realizing that they were willing to work hard and do anything he asked them to do, he decided to keep them on board the ship.

After a long sail trip they finally arrived in Philadelphia, USA. That was a big surprise as they were hoping to end up in Australia. They were both transferred to prison, where they would have to stay until authorities decided to ship them back home. Neither one of them could speak a word of English. They finally located a Finish speaking person, who could talk to the boys and help with the translation. Then they found out that the one guy was married, so arrangements were made, to send him back to Finland.

Leo knew that he had an uncle by the name of Westerberg living somewhere in the USA. They found uncle Axel Westerberg, He was able to get Leo out of prison and Leo was then sent to Canada to get the proper visa and necessary papers in order for him to come back to the USA legally. Our uncle was then able to sponsor his nephew.

LEA'S SUMMER HOUSE

LEA AND ME AFTER SOUNA

MAJ'S ISLAND

SUMMER SOLSTICE
ON "JERVO"

DINNER AT SUMMER HOUSE

Eila

GOSTA, EILA AND SYLVIA
EATING AGAIN IN EILA'S
SUMMERHOUSE

GERD AND EILA

LEARNING TO ROLL
OUT FLATBREAD

As I mentioned earlier, Leo was a very adventurous individual and always wanted to learn to fly. He joined the American Army. He was a crew chief on board one of the military planes for a while and signed up to become a paratrooper. He had several "streamers" while jumping out of planes, but fortunately managed to survive every one of them with just a few bruises and one broken leg. He also had a military tour in Germany while he was in the US Army.

Leo had a lot of "close calls" in his life, which he survived, and he was very thankful for the fact that he survived all of them. He therefore became a very good Christian in his retirement days.

He was married to a lovely girl, Mildred, from North Caroline and they had 2 children, a daughter, Eila, and a son Hobart Finn. They are both still living in USA. Eila is living in Alabama and Hobart is living in New Mexico.

LEO AND MILDRED

EILA

A couple of years after Leo was born my Mom was pregnant again for the sixth time. This time it was Eila's turn to see the world. She was born September 24, 1931.

She was one of the five siblings from our family who was sent to Sweden together with Lea, Leo, Gunnel and me in 1939. Fortunately we didn't stay there very long as that part of the war only lasted 100 days.

Eila and Gunnel decided to move to Sweden when they were teen-agers. They were going to try to find some jobs in Stockholm, which they did. Exactly what they were doing, I don't know.

Gunnel went back to Finland, but Eila stayed in Sweden, as she had met a young man, Gosta, whom she later married.

They settled down in a small town, Umeaa, in the northern part of Sweden. She is still living in Umeaa, although her husband, Gosta passed away several years ago. They had two children, Gothe and Gerd, They are both still living in Sweden.

Over the years she has had several medical problems like stomach and colon cancer. She had an operation for colon cancer in 2006, when I went to visit her in Umeaa. She has since been suffering with leg problems, which she tends to blame for the surgery she had at that time. She is now moving around with the help of her walker. She proudly calls it her "Rouladen".

Eila and Sylvia, together with Sylvia's first baby, Annele, were the first two sisters from my Finish family, who came to visit me in Denmark after I had been sent there in 1941.

EILA, SYLVIA AND ANNELE VISITING IN DENMARK

ENJOYING THE TRIP IN THE HYDROFOIL

EILA CELEBRATING HER BIRTHDAY

FAMILY GATHERING AT THE SUMMERHOUSE

SYLVIA JEANETTE, MAJ, SVEN, LEA & GUNNEL

GUNNEL

Gunnel was my youngest sister and the second youngest sibling in the group. She was born in 1933.

I used to think of Gunnel as my "little" sister, even though she was five years older than I. Perhaps because, at one time she was shorter than I was. It appears that I know even less about her than any of my other siblings. Our sister, Sylvia, who was an office manager for a well known company in Helsinki, arranged for Gunnel to get a job at the same company as her, and she worked there for several years.

Just like the rest of the family, she loved cats, and had several of them.

She married a young man, Toivo in 1952.

They only had one child, a Daughter, who I never got to know.

Evidently their marriage was not a happy one and Gunnel developed a drinking problem.

Needless to say, they ended up having a divorce.

Unfortunately, Gunnel died at a fairly young age.

JEANETTE AND GUNNEL

ARRIVING IN DENMARK

In December of 1941, at the age of three (3), I was the only member of my family, who was sent away. This time I was sent to Denmark.

The war between Finland and Russia had started again, and the Finish government saw no other choice, than to send the youngest children out of the Country again.

Only a few children had been sent to Denmark in 1939 as the war only lasted for 3 months. Of course there were a lot of debate going on between the parents and the government whether it was the right thing to do.

The majority of the younger children were sent out of Finland in 1941, when I also was sent away. There were 3500-4000 children sent to Denmark at that time.

The water can be very rough in the Baltic Bay, especially in the winter time. On the boat trip from Turku (Aabo) to Stockholm a lot of the children were sea sick and so were most of the nurses.

We were escorted by Finish nurses on the longest part of the trip. When we arrived in Copenhagen they were relieved by Danish nurses. We were all very tired after the long trip, which had taken several days.

Right away we were sent to some centers where Doctors and nurses were busy examining all of us and giving us medical check ups, chest X-rays, checking for tuberculosis and making sure that we were not bringing in any contagious illnesses. Any child, who might have had signs of illness or colds was hospitalized.

It took several days before we could be sent on to the different families, who had volunteered to take care of a Finish child.

After a couple of days I was placed on a train together with some of the other children. Things seemed very confusing and frightening and people were now talking another language again. Besides, I had no idea where I was going and what was going to happen to me.

I remember thinking that I just wanted to go back home to my Mom & Dad. I could feel the tears welling up in my eyes, but I had to be brave.

I finally arrived in a small town called Haslev, which was south of Copenhagen. There we were met by a lot of anxious people. I was wishing: "I just want to hide somewhere".

We were escorted out of the train and taken across the street from the railroad station to a hotel where we were brought into a large ball room. I was told to sit down on the floor. I found a place in the corner together with some of the kids about the same age as I. We were handed a small glass of

"TOKEN OF THANKS" FROM FINLAND TO DANISH FAMILIES FOR ALL THEIR HELP DURING THE WAR

 TOKEN

THE EMBLEMS THE DANISH FAMILIES RECEIVED FROM FINLAND AS A "THANK YOU TOKEN" FOR SAVING THE CHILDREN.

THE OLTHAVER FAMILY

"SORTEPER" SLEEPING WITH ME

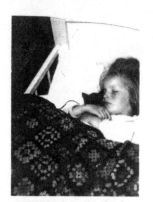

JEANETTE

JEANETTE AT AGE 3-4-5

juice and a few cookies. The families who wanted to pick up a child were all coming into the room as well. They were looking at all those scared, tired and confused kids sitting there.

My Mom had given me a little red suitcase, which I carefully was holding on to. She told me to take very good care of it and not lose it, as it was my only possession. It contained some very "important" items. A half naked black doll, a 2-3 days old sandwich, a couple of crackers and some gloves. I was not going to let go of my beautiful red suitcase.

One little boy sitting next to me had decided that he liked it too and wanted to get my suitcase, so we started a "Tuck-O-war". I was not going to let him run off with my only and special possession. I started to cry and hitting him, so he finally gave in and I got to keep my suitcase. I still had that suitcase several years later.

Out of the almost 4000 Finish children who were sent to Denmark only 58 arrived in Haslev.

Two of the people that had gathered to meet those scared and confused little kids were a gentleman Anton Olthaver and his daughter Bente. They turned out to be part of the family I was to stay with. They had volunteered to take a little girl for a short while. Nobody knew exactly how long that was going to be.

The family that I stayed with was an elderly couple with two children, a son, Arne and a daughter, whose name was Bente.

They were both a lot older than me. Arne was 17 years old and Bente was 14 years old. I was told later that it was Bente's idea to adopt a Finish kid. My new "step Mom" was Dagmar. She definitely turned out to be the disciplinarian of the two parents.

When Anton and Bente came to pick me up at the hotel ball room, he took one look around at all the kids and jokingly mentioned to Bente: "I sure hope we don't get that cute little girl with the big ski boots". Well, that little girl was me. The boots that had been passed down from one . . . . or several of my older sisters, were several sizes too big, but they kept my feet warm. The hat and coat I was wearing had been sown by my sister Sylvia, so I looked very presentable.

The original plans were that the children were just supposed to stay in Denmark for 2 to 6 months. However, the oldest of the children were sent back home after a couple of months for school and work, even though the war was still going on.

After the initial paper signing and making sure everybody got the right child, Anton and Bente drove me home to their house in Jernbanegade, the main street in Haslev. They were both trying to talk to me, but I didn't understand a word they said. Since they knew that I was exhausted and upset they first tried to give me something to eat, but I was not hungry, so I was put to bed in what became my own room. I spent all night crying my heart out. Evidently that same scene was repeating itself night after night until they got one of the Finish nurses to come to the house to help, translate and explain that I was afraid to sleep by myself. I was used to sleeping with my Mom. After all I was just 3 years old.

My new "step Mom" Dagmar decided to get me a little kitten, which I called "Sorteper". It was so sweet and soft. They let the cat sleep with me in the bed every night. Now I had some one to love and hug. I loved that kitty and it made me feel wanted again.

The family tried very hard to make me feel comfortable and at ease. I knew they were doing it out of love.

After some time I started to feel more comfortable and relaxed. I very quickly learned the language. Since I already spoke Swedish, it was easier for me because there are a lot of similarities between the two languages.

I soon found a couple of kids to play with. The first one was Egon, who lived in the same building as me. His family was renting one of the apartments in that building.

He was a very sweet boy, about the same age as I was. We had a lot of fun playing together and when I got a tricycle, we would try to race each other on the bikes.

I later on got to know a girl Sonja, who lived across the street from me. I will tell you more about her later in this book.

ME AND EGON

MY DANISH FAMILY

Initially I referred to my Danish family as my "Step Family". In fact, they became actually more family to me than my real Finish family, as I spent most of my life with them. They were able to take better care of me during that time and especially under the circumstances.

My Dad, ("Far", as I later started to call him) had a few houses and apartment buildings on the main street. He and the family were occupying one of those apartments. He had an electric firm and a store in the same building with electrical appliances, lamps and other electronic items. Far was a very kind and good hearted person. He was the kind of person who would "give his shirt off his back" to anybody who needed help. It was obvious that money was never any of his main concerns. Often when there had been a major sale of something in his business or some big electric job had been performed for some of his clients, he was never concerned about getting the payment paid on time and in some cases it was never collected.

Even though he had a book keeper, who obviously didn't do a very good job, people still owed him money. Therefore he ended up having a Tax problem, as the taxes were not always paid on time.

Far had a blue Opel Cadet car, which had a big loud-speaker installed on the roof of the car. It was being used to provide music and announcements at different events like fares and other events going on from time to time around town.

When Arne, my brother was old enough, he was the one who was taking care of that part of the business.

My Dad also had two convertible Renault cars, which he used for transportation to work most of the time. He always had the roof down, so he could get lots of "Fresh air", as he said, even during the cold winter months. We thought they were funny looking, so they were called "The bath tubs". There were times during the war years, when none of the cars could be used due to lack of gasoline, so then they had to be put up on blocks in the garage for long periods of time.

THE OLTHAVER FAMILY

DAGMAR AND ME AT THE BEACH

THE OPEL WITH THE LOUDSPEAKER

ANTON

MAJ AND NILS VISITING
IN DENMARK

DAGMAR

ROYAL PALACE

THE PARLIAMENT BUILDING, (Sven's House)

JEANETTE IN THE (SPEAKER'S CHAIR)

TUTA & SEPPO

MY DANISH FAMILY.
(MOR)

My Danish mother, Dagmar, was not a healthy individual.

She wanted me to call her "Mor" (Mom) which I did.

When she was a child she had a bad accident falling down some stairs and had therefore developed leg and back problems which were still paining her. Because of her illness and pain she could be very unreasonable and unfair. Often she would forbid me to go with my friends to see a movie, or go to birthday parties and later on, to dances or other functions I might have been invited to. Needless to say, that was upsetting and made me unhappy. Those were some of the times I wished I could just go back to my family in Finland again.

She was, however, a very talented person. She could do almost anything she wanted to do with her hands, i.e.

knitting, crocheting, sewing, crosstiching and embroidering as well as other forms of art and crafts.

A lot of my dresses had beautiful hand embroidery sewn on to them when I was younger. Some of my sweaters were knitted with very colorful designs and patterns, which were often admired by other people.

My Mom was also an excellent pianist. She decided that I should also learn to play the piano, but at that time I was not very interested in having to practice playing the piano every day.

The Piano teacher came to the house once or twice a week to teach me, but usually they could not find me as I was hiding somewhere, either at my girl friends house or in the garden hanging up side down in my trapeze or rings. They knew that was my favorite place to be. I always felt safe there and "on top of the world".

My Mom finally gave up trying to get me interested in the piano playing. Of course now I wish that I had taken some interest in learning to play.

Even though my new Mom and Dad were both very caring people, they were not particularly warm individuals. I never saw them hugging or kissing each other. I never received a reassuring pat on the back or got a hug when I had done something good. I would have welcomed a hug from any of them any time. I think any child would love that.

My Mom was definitely the disciplinarian of the two.

She had a long wooden shoe horn, which was used by my Dad to put his shoes or boots on. She decided that it could also be used as a paddle on me when I was bad. Whenever I got in trouble or was naughty, it would be used on me for a spanking.

One day, when I thought that I had had enough of that, I decided that I was going to "teach her a lesson". So I decided to hide the shoe horn some where. The best place I could find was under the dining room table. The table had extensions in both ends. I found out that the horn could just fit and stay under the table, as long as it wasn't pulled out.

Unfortunately one day shortly after my little "game" we were having a dinner party and the table had to be extended to full size.

Guess what? The shoe horn fell out on the floor and I knew I was in serious trouble!

My Mom right away thought she had better use "The paddle" now, so I started running around the table with her right behind me. Fortunately for me she was not very fast, so before we knew it I was behind her.

I started to giggle and soon she was laughing as well. We were both laughing so hard that we had to stop running and sit down.

My Grandmother lived in a house further up the main street. That house also belonged to the Olthaver family. Her back yard was full of fruit trees, like apples, pears, plums and cherries.

My girl friend Sonja and I often went up to taste some of the fruit. We found out that not only did they taste good, but we could also make a business out of selling the fruit to other people and make a lot of money. So we started our business by setting up a table and chairs in front of our house and opened a fruit and juice stand.

We had a very good business going until Grandma found out where all of her fruit was disappearing.

We climbed the trees and picked all the fruit we could reach . . . . The only problem was that we forgot to ask for Grandma's permission. When she found most of her fruit gone she was furious. We knew we were in a lot of trouble, when she put a stop to our business.

ARNE, ELSE, MIE, AND ANKER

ANKER AND ME

ELSE AND ARNE CELEBRATING THEIR GOLDEN ANNIVERSARY

ARNE

My Danish "step brother", Arne and "step sister" Bente were quite a bit older than me. He was 17 years old and Bente was 14 years old when I came to Denmark as a 3 years old. There were no other children in the family about my age that I could play with, but that was OK since it didn't take long before I found some kids my own age.

Arne had a very good job as an Electro Engineer working at SEAS, (Sydostsjaellands Electricitets Actieselskab). He was very smart and knowledgably in his field, but his talent didn't stop there.

He tried his hands and talents in a lot of other directions. He built an R.V. Camper by himself. He and his wife, Else, traveled several trips around Europe in this camper. He also built a couple of row boats, which they took down to Fakse Ladeplads to play with and enjoyed rowing around in. He even tried to sew clothing and made a beautiful dress for his wife. That was a short lived experience.

Arne's biggest accomplishment was when he became very instrumental in the rebuilding of the major Radio-Computer system for SEAS.

He had built his own radio-computer system, which took up all of one room in his house. Through that he was able to communicate with other computer operators in different parts of the world like Brazil, Africa and other parts of Europe long before most people even knew of that possibility.

Arne and Else had two children, a son, Anker and a daughter, AnneMarie, who goes by the name "Mie". Anker and his wife Susie still live in the same house where I lived and grew up, while I was in Haslev, Denmark.

Unfortunately, Arne developed some heart or respiratory illness. I believe it was primarily epicarditis or some form of heart problems. Arne passed away in January, 1999.

ELSE AND THE KIDS

MIE (ARNE'S DAUGHTER) AND ME

ANKER, SUSIE, MIE, ELSE

ARNE AND ANKER WASHING DISHES

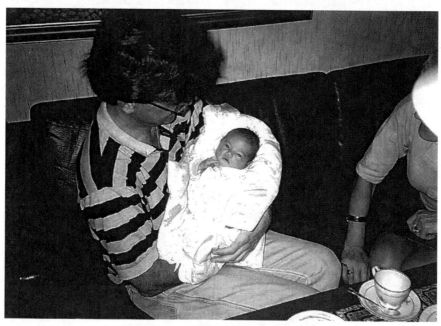

ANKER WITH HIS NEW BABY

BENTE & ELSE

TORBEN & BENTE

TORBEN, ALEX AND FINN

BENTE AND ME

BENTE

Bente was also very talented. She turned out to be a very gifted artist. She was particularly very good at painting oil paintings of portraits and flower arrangements. She also enjoyed working on ceramics. She painted a complete coffee and tea sets. I think that one of her three sons still has the sets.

Bente was also a very good seamstress. She loved knitting and was determined to teach me the different patterns and color combinations. I did learn to knit, but never really enjoyed it the way she did. Besides, my back and neck muscles would tighten up. I would get so tense that it was uncomfortable. She had fun trying all sorts of stitchery and was very good at all forms of hand work.

She later on opened her own arts and craft studio, where she was able to sell all her own work.

Neither Arne nor Bente were much in to physical fitness in the way of exercising or dancing. Bente did become an excellent swimmer and participated in several swim meets around the Country.

Unfortunately, she became a very heavy cigarette smoker, which affected her health. She started having some respiratory and back problems. She had several back surgeries and even though two of her three sons and one daughter in law were all physicians, they were unable to correct the problem. She suffered for several years with severe back pain and died in February, 2001.

Bente and her former husband had three sons, Finn, Torben and Alex. All three of them still live in the Copenhagen area.

FINN, ALEX AND TORBEN

BENTE, ME AND DAGMAR   RUTH, ME AND KAREN

BEACH & POOL FUN

EBBA & ME   EGON AND I ARE WORKING

RUTH AND ME

ANNELE JEANETTE AT DIFFERENT AGES

ME, LITTLE ANNELE AND ELSE

ANNELE AND ANNELI

EILA, SYLVIA, LITTLE ANNELE
WITH THE OLTHAVER FAMILY

AGE FOUR

At age 4, I started to attend dance, gymnastic and acrobatic classes . . . Mor and Far, as I was now calling them, soon realized that I was very flexible and agile, so I was first enrolled in a gymnastic class. I loved exercising and I already spent most of my time doing hand stands and "Sawmosaltes". Pretty soon I was able to "tie knots" on my body, always doing head stands, hand stands or balancing on something. I needed to go even further, so I started in ballet and tap classes as well. That was just "my style". It was like I couldn't get enough activities of that kind.

When it was time for recitals and shows, I was often chosen to do several solo numbers and I loved it. It also made me feel a lot more confident as I was a shy kid.

I guess my real Mother was not kidding when she said "She was already dancing *before* she was born".

I was always involved in some type of dance activity. Later, during my elementary school years, I was learning to dance "Square Dance" at the school and Ballroom Dancing in a dance class.

Exercise and dancing has always been a very important part of my life.

When I was a child I already decided that I was going to be a dance, gymnastic and ballet instructor, which I did do later on. I taught Dance-works, Jas-aerobics and Ballet for over twenty five years.

I had somewhere seen a very sophisticated gymnastic set with a trapeze, rings and a couple of swings. I begged my Dad to buy me a set like that. He got me a wonderful set, which was installed in the back of the garden. Now I had my favorite "escape area". That was where I would usually be hiding, when I wanted to be alone or get away "from the World", when it was time for piano practice or if I had been a bad girl.

I loved music and singing, but not practicing the piano. Of course as an adult person I often wished that I had taken advantage of that opportunity when I was younger.

THE GERMAN OCCUPATION
OF DENMARK

During the years I had been living in Denmark, Germany had been occupying Denmark, and sending lots of army troops up through the Country. Germany had taken over most of the schools and major companies. The schools were turned in to "Lazarettos", which was hospitals for all the wounded German soldiers. Some times you could see a young German soldier walking down the street, perhaps with part of an arm or leg missing, or other visible injuries. I didn't like to see that at all.

Even though life seemed somewhat normal, there was still a war going on. Staples such as beef, pork and chicken could only be bought with certain coupons. Vegetables and fruit, which were usually imported from other countries were very scarce and hard to get and dairy products were very limited.

As a young child I was obviously not concerned about getting enough food or things for the family during the war. My parents had to taking care of that part.

Everybody was instructed to get black curtains and blinds for the windows and roll them down every night. Once in a while you could hear the sirens blowing. That would alert you that planes were overhead and might be bombing somewhere or that we might be under attack.

If you were out of the house and walking on the street, you might get stopped by the military police and escorted to a bomb shelter somewhere, maybe far away from your home. Of course, that would make every body very nervous, especially when you could hear planes over head, with shooting going on and bombs blasting.

SONJA

S onja was a little "Squirt" with lots of energy and crazy ideas. We soon found out that we had a lot in common. We could have a lot of fun and get in to trouble together. She was the youngest and only girl in her family with 3 older brothers. Sonja was a bit of a "tomboy" and I soon became one also.

Sonja's Dad was a goldsmith. He had a goldsmith/jewelry business and her Mother often helped out in the store. The nanny/live in maid was supposed to watch Sonja and her brothers. She was not overly watchful of the children, so Sonja and I had plenty of opportunity to get in to trouble. For the most part, it took place in their house or yard.

The Larsen's had a big back yard and in the back part of the yard the military had built a bunker, which was used during the war time. It was security center for protection during bomb attacks. The center was not being used most of the time, so we thought it could be used as a "play hospital".

We gathered some of the neighborhood kids and played hospital with them. I was the doctor and Sonja was my nurse.

We had to use flash lights or candles to light up as there were no electric lights. Under those conditions it was not easy to perform "serious operations".

Most of the time the other kids didn't find it as interesting and amusing as we did. Especially when we bandaged them up too much or poked them with sticks for "injections".

One day Sonja and I decided to try to jump from the top of a tall cabinet on to her parent's bed. Unfortunately it was not like the stack of mattresses we used in the guest room and one of my jumps collapsed the bed.

Needless to say her Dad got furious when he found out how it collapsed and who did it. I was sent home with the orders: "Don't come back again any time soon". I had heard that a few times before, so I was embarrassed, but not afraid. I was back playing with Sonja again the next day!

On one of my Birthdays I had received a large doll carriage, which I loved. I played with it a lot. Since Sonja was small, we found out that she could fit into the carriage. We pretended she was my "Baby". I put her in the doll carriage; put a blanket over her and a pacifier in her mouth. When people wanted to see my "Baby" and they saw Sonja lying there, we would all "explode" in laughter.

I obviously spent a lot of time with Sonja and in the Larsen household, especially the first few years. I loved being there playing with Sonja and her brothers. Besides the house keeper/nanny who was supposed to keep track of what was going on at the house and to watch the kids, was not paying much attention to what the kids were doing. We had a lot of opportunity and liberty to do anything we wanted to do.

Both their parents were usually busy working at the jewelry store or with their gold smith business.

I thought it was perfect that we could just get into lots of fun stuff and do what we wanted. We did things that were not allowed at my house.

On the 3rd. floor of the Larsen house were a couple of extra guest rooms, which were usually unoccupied. In one of these rooms were some old mattresses stacked on top of each other. We decided to use those mattresses like a trampoline. After a lot of practice jumps we became a couple of expert "Trampoline Artists".

Once in a while we would let her brother, Kai, join us in our fun game mainly to prevent him from telling their parents what we were doing. We knew that it could be a problem if they knew about our new game. I am not sure what those mattresses looked like by the time we were finished using them. I don't think they would be too comfortable to sleep on. But for us they served a great purpose.

SONJA AND ME

SONJA

SONJA AND ME

MY DOLL CARRIAGE
AND ME

VISITING SONJA, BEND ROSKILDE

THE TRIP TO
THE COUNTRYSIDE

I thoroughly enjoyed playing in the snow. In the winter time, when we had received a large snow fall and the ground was covered with white powdery stuff, I would either be skiing or skating.

In the northern part of Haslev was a small pond where we could go skating, and that was usually covered by a lot of skating kids.

Denmark is a rather flat country, When you go skiing, it is strictly cross country skiing. You have to travel to another country like Norway or Sweden, maybe south to the Alps, to do down hill skiing and slalom.

One winter, some of the older boys from the Gymnasium, had constructed "Make believe ski jumps" in the woods for anybody who wanted to try the jumps. There were three different heights: low, medium and high.

I was usually rather daring when there was a chance to try something new. So I decided, since I was very athletic, to try the highest one of the jumps. My skis were not slalom or down hill skis, but ordinary cross country skis. They were just made of wood and not designed for jumping.

Unfortunately, when I jumped, I managed to break both skis in several places. When I came home with the broken pieces, my parents were furious. I didn't get to go skiing for a long time after that.

Everybody who has tried to drive a car in snow conditions knows how difficult and dangerous it can be, particularly if part of the snow has been melting and turned to ice. Therefore, when the farmers had to go to the city for shopping or other business, they would sometimes arrive in a horse drawn sledge or buggy instead of driving.

I had often thought how much fun it could be to hang on to one of those sledges and get a free ride somewhere.

Sonja and I decided to try that one day. When we saw one coming down the main street we grabbed the chance, and ran to hang on to the sledge. We didn't know the man, who was riding in it, but he didn't see us.

Before we knew it, we found ourselves many miles outside town, and neither one of us had given any thought to how to get back home again. We had no idea where we were. We could see a farm, somewhere in a distance, but we decided to head back the way we came.

We thought of calling home, to let our families know, where we were. Maybe somebody would come and pick us up, but then we would have to walk even further to get to the farm.

91

It was late in the afternoon, when we started out, so we knew it might be very late, maybe evening, before we would get home. Sonja didn't have a watch, and neither did I.

At that time we didn't have cell phones either.

It was a long way to walk, sometimes in high snow drifts. The weather was getting colder. We were getting tired and it was now late and darker.

Our parents were getting very concerned, as they didn't know where we were. Of course, we had not told them, what we were up to.

They would never have agreed to us taking that "fun trip".

They got very angry when we told them, where we had been, but they were happy that we made it home safely.

SKIING

INGE WITH HER TWINS

ERICA WITH HER CHILDREN

ERICA & HUSBAND

STARTING SCHOOL

When I was seven (7) years old I started to attend school.

I soon became good friends with another girl, Inge, who was in the same class as I was. We found out that we had a lot in common. I loved gymnastics', dancing and acrobatics and so did she. Neither one of us was very interested in learning to read or write yet, so instead of paying attention to school and home work, we would have fun playing in our rings and trapeze or even go swimming. We didn't find ball playing much fun either. Unfortunately we were both a couple of gigglers. It often resulted in us being sent outside the class room or we were placed in chairs far away from each other in the room. When it was time to move up to the next grade the teacher decided to place us in separate class rooms.

Unfortunately that "back fired", as it sent us both into stages of depression, unable to sleep and unwilling to eat.

The families, both Inge's and mine, realized that it was becoming a serious situation. They all got together and ended up having meetings with the principal and teachers.

After realizing that the separation was not helping any of us, they finally agreed to place us both back into the same class room again. Life was once again "looking up" and Inge and I stayed in the same classes until I was uprooted one more time and moved away from my friends. I was still good friends with Sonja, but didn't spent as much time together with her as I had earlier.

ANNELE READY FOR SCHOOL

REALCLASSEN, HASLEV GYMNASIUM

BIRTHDAY PARTY

BIRTHDAY PARTY

"MAYDAY" FLOAT

INGE, PHIL AND POUL

LUNCH IN THE GARDEN

SUSIE AND ME

THE GARDEN

T he garden in the back yard of the house in Haslev was definitely one of the greatest places "to hang out", even when I wasn't hanging up side down in my new exercise set. The garden was quiet and very beautiful. It was landscaped with lots of special trees, many colorful bushes and plants. There were even some large pine trees, which had been sent down from Finland. There was a little fish pond, which could sometimes double as a nice basin, where we could cool our feet, on hot days.

In one of the corners was an outdoor fire place. It could also be used as a barbeque. There were a couple of picnic sets and lounge chairs in different places.

The garden house was often used by me and my friends to play in. It was small, but a perfect size for us. It had a sofa, table and a couple of chairs, besides when it was raining, most of my toys were usually stored there. Next to the garden house was a hothouse, "drivhus", where some vegetables and grape plants were kept.

In the summer time the family often invited friends and neighbors to join us for coffee or lunch in the garden. I thought it was so "hyggeligt", cozy and we always had a good time.

THE GARDEN

FOUNTAIN IN TIVOLI

LEAVING DENMARK

When the 2nd. World War ended in 1945 all the parents and the Finish Government wanted to bring home all the children, which were still situated in Sweden, Norway and Denmark.

I had been living with the family in Denmark for four (4) years now. I was speaking fluent Danish and had forgotten how to speak Finnish. I had just started school and had settled in very well with the Danish family and my little friends. To be uprooted again was very difficult and upsetting.

It had been a long time, (four years), since I had seen or talked to my own family. There had been very little communication between the family in Denmark and my birth family in Finland. I hardly remembered my parents and siblings. They almost seamed like strangers now and we no longer spoke the same language.

The week-end before I was due to leave Denmark to go back to Finland, my Dad, Anton had decided that we were going to have a very special day with a fancy dinner in Copenhagen. He had made reservations at a restaurant called

"Palmehaven". It was a very beautiful restaurant decorated with several palm trees and tropical plant arrangements. It also had a huge stage where a dinner show took place and you could see famous artists performing. Unfortunately, I don't think the restaurant is there any more. It was supposed to be a fun and enjoyable day for all of us, but it turned out to be a day with very mixed emotions.

I started feeling sick while we were having dinner. I could not eat my food and ended up spending most of the evening in the bathroom. When I returned to the table again I almost slept through the rest of the evening. I don't even remember anything about the dinner show.

Perhaps I had eaten something that didn't agree with me, ... or maybe it was because I was nervous and sad about leaving the family, friends and the life I had become accustomed to in Denmark.

Before we went to the restaurant we were walking around the City and did some shopping. One of the things that I had seen and fell in love with was a doll I saw in a store window. My Dad bought the doll for me to brighten my day and that made me very happy.

I also got a pair of white shoes. They were the greatest looking shoes I had ever seen. Of course I had to wear them right away. The only problem was that they were too small for my feet and they were just "killing" me, while I was walking in them. But I wasn't about to tell my family about that problem. I had insisted that they were just perfect when I got them, and they were the only ones of that kind the store had.

The day that I now again had to leave my Danish family and all my little friends behind had arrived. I was afraid that I might never see Anton, Dagmar, Arne, Bente, Sonja, Inge or any of my little friends again. I think I was trying to 'block out' most of the time & things that was happening during those days because, quite frankly, I don't remember very much about what really happened during that period.

The Olthaver family was also very sorry to see me leave them. They had gotten used to have this little fun loving kid around for such a long time.

USPENSKI CATHEDRAL
(STATUE: ALEXANDER II)

ANTON VISITING
IN FINLAND
WITH ME, ATTI, MAJ,
RAY AND KENNETH

FINISH LANDSCAPE

"TEMPELPLATS CHURCH" OPENED 1969.
(Cut in to the mountain)
(CAPACATY: 740 PEOPLE)

OLYMPIC STADIUM

BACK IN FINLAND

My family in Finland was anxious and happy to have me back home.

I was definitely having mixed feelings leaving the family in Denmark, but at the same time was anxious to see my real family again.

When I came back to Helsinki, I found both my parents working every day and all my sisters and brothers attending school. I was primarily left to my own devices. They were all gone during the day, so I was left by myself in the apartment in Snellmansgatan. Even though I was seven years old I didn't start school right away.

There were no other kids in the immediate neighborhood. I was feeling bored and started feeling home sick for Denmark.

One day I decided to go out looking for my Mother, even though I didn't know my way around the City or where to start looking for her. I got thoroughly lost.

In the meantime my sisters had arrived home from school and realized that I was gone. They called my Mom and Dad as well as the police and told them that I was missing. Of course a search was started.

Finally the police found me after several hours wandering aimlessly around Helsinki, tired, scared, cold and hungry. Needless to say I was very happy to see the whole family again.

My Mom and Dad were afraid that I had actually run away from home. For a long time after that they still insisted that they were right about that. I don't think so, but I am not so sure who was the right ones any more. They knew that I was feeling very lonely most of the time since the whole family was gone during the day.

It didn't take long for my parents to realize that I was becoming more and more unhappy.

My ability to speak the Finnish language was long gone. There were no other small children to play with and my two youngest sisters Gunnel and Eila were in school and my older sisters were all gone most of the days. There was nothing for me to do while they were away.

Since I had been gone from the family for four years as a three years old child, I had developed new customs and habits. Everybody in the family was now that much older and we really didn't know each other the same way any more.

My language was Danish and my family spoke mostly Finish and sometimes Swedish, which I, at least could understand.

My parents, Aiti and Isa (Finish for Mom & Dad) had together with Maj, my oldest sister come to the conclusion that I probably would be much happier living in Denmark, where I already had spent most of my life.

MAJ, NILS AND KENNETH

RAY, MAJ AND NILS

My Danish Mom and Dad had already requested and asked if they could have me come back to Denmark and stay there.

Unfortunately my Danish Mom became very ill after I had left the Danish family. In the meantime I had become homesick for the life I had been used to while living with the Olthaver family and my little friends in Haslev. It was then agreed by both families that I could again travel back to Denmark to stay providing that I would travel home to Finland once a year or at least every other year.

My oldest sister, Maj traveled with me to Denmark and my Danish "Far" came to Stockholm, Sweden to meet us and we all continued together to Copenhagen.

When we arrived in Copenhagen the rest of the family together with my first little girl friend Sonja were meeting us at the Airport with Danish and Finish flags. I was so excited and happy to see them all again and I could see they were too. There were a lot of happy faces and tears being shed.

SYLVIA EXERCISING

DANISH CITIZEN

Since I had been back in Denmark for several years and my parents had given the Danish family permission to keep me there, providing that I could travel back to Finland once a year or at least every other year to visit my own family, the family in Denmark decided that it was probably time for me to become a Danish Citizen. They never "forced the issue" and never said: "You have to be a Danish Citizen now". They left it up to me to decide if that was what I wanted to do. Since I already felt like I was more Danish than Finish, I decided that the time was right.

October 27, 1960 was the chosen date. There were no big "Fanfare" planned, but it was still a special day for me. I was now a Danish Citizen.

After I had returned to Denmark the summer of 1946, the Olthaver family had already decided that they wanted to adopt me as their daughter. They decided that it would call for a special celebration, so August 27, 1947 was the special day for me to be adopted. We were having a very nice dinner party with close friend and family. I was permitted to add Olthaver to my name. My name was now Annele Jeanette Selander Olthaver.

MENTOR

When somebody asks you: "Who is your mentor?". You sometimes have to stop and think, who is the person who has been the most influential "advise giver" aside from your parents, I will have to say George, He was an adult person, who had one son a little older than me. George obviously liked children a lot and somehow he became a very good friend.

As a child I would go down to his shop almost every day and talk to him. He was always willing to listen to whatever I had to say. Even though he was a very busy man, He always took time to listen to your complaints or whatever you had to talk to him about and give me his advice. I always felt very comfortable talking to him about anything which might have been troubling me, especially things I could not talk to my Mother or Father about.

MY CONFIRMATION

When I was 14 years old I started to attend Catechism as the preparation for my confirmation, as I was being confirmed in Haslev Church.

Unfortunately, my class mates were not being confirmed at the same time but later on. I could not understand why I couldn't wait to be confirmed together with them, which definitely were my wishes. I was hoping and praying that I could get my Mom and Dad to change their minds, but without any luck.

My Mom was very stubborn and very set in her ways about everything. My Finish, birth, parents were invited to come down to Denmark for my confirmation. Needless to say, I was very pleased about that.

It was just wonderful to see them again.

The confirmation itself was very festive. I had a big dinner party with sit-down-dinner for 30-some guests. We had a 6 course dinner with different wines and beautiful decorations.

I was dressed in a long white gown, and the highlight for me was the big table filled with all the presents I had received from family and friends for my confirmation.

The Scandinavians have a very nice tradition when they are celebrating confirmations, christenings, weddings and other big celebrations, to have different sing-alongs about the people who are being celebrated.

I found out later why the family wanted me to be confirmed before my class mates. Anton and Dagmar had decided to move to Nykobing Falster and I had to move with them. I would much rather stay with my friends in Haslev and continue my studying in Haslev Gymnasium and graduate there, but they had already made up their mind about the move.

Once again I had to leave my good friends behind.

I was never told the reason why they were moving to Nykobing Falster. The whole thing seemed a bit like a mystery. I think they had a problem with the tax charges on the business and the buildings, which they still owned, and are still owned by the Olthaver family.

They didn't stay in Nykobing very long, only for a couple of years and then they moved back to Haslev again.

I didn't particularly like living in Nykobing, but I soon got to know some new friends and graduated from High School there.

My Sister Bente and her husband also lived in Nykobing, so that was nice. But I was happy when we all moved back to Haslev again.

"ATTI", ME AND "ISA"

FAR, ME AND MOR

ANNELE JEANETTE

CONFIRMATION PARTY

117

NIKE

JEANETTE EXERCISING

MY LIFE IN NYKOBING FALSTER

While living and attending school in Nykobing, I started doing a little "dating", mainly with some of the boys in my own classes. I had developed a "crush" on one of my girl friends older brother, but unfortunately he was not interested in me.

At a very inopportune time, while I was at my girl friend's house, he remarked that I was getting "a little round", which to me translated as I was "Getting FAT". That was the last thing I wanted to be, so I decided to go on a starvation diet. I simply stopped eating, which, of course, was very stupid. I lost a lot of weight and was getting very skinny. It resulted in me missing my period for a couple of years and I could tell that I was definitely getting weaker, but I wanted to be *thin*.

I didn't know that there was actually a name "Anorexia" for this condition. My Dad soon realized that I was not eating, but starving myself. He then ordered me to "EAT, or you might get sick".

I started eating again, but would then just go to the bath room and throw all my food up. It had now turned in to the illness "Bulimia".

Fortunately for me, my friends started to tell me that I was "looking terrible", and that I could get very sick and kill myself if I continued, so little by little I started to come to my senses and got back on a regular eating habit again.

In 1952 I joined an athletic club by the name "NIKE" in Nykobing, as my dance, gymnastic and ballet activities had for the time taken a "back seat" since I had moved to Nykobing however I still wanted to be active together with my friends. We had a lot of various athletic activities and fun week-end trips.

Since everybody knew that I was born in Helsinki, Finland and the Olympic Games were going to be celebrated the summer of 1952 in Helsinki, I was chosen to help carry the Olympic Torch through part of Denmark, so I was running the torch part of the way from Nykobing Falster to the bridge connecting Falster and Sjaelland (Sealand). The Olympic Torch was to be transported from Greece all the way north to Helsinki, Finland.

I was very happy to have that experience and be part of this piece of history as it was quite an honor.

However, at the time I didn't think it was "any big deal", I found out, later that it actually was, once I read the papers and saw the photos.

EMBLEM FROM HELSINKI OLYMPICS

Byskolens realister i Nykøbing F.: I bageste række fra venstre: Svend Hansen, Knud Erik Olsen, Leo Larsen, Jørn Rasmussen, Ivar Hellebjerg Mads Gode, Flemming Rasmussen, Knud Jensen. Siddende: Bonni Martensen, Annele Olthaver, lærerinde frk. G. Sørensen, Anna Rasmussen, Bodil Hansen, Ingrid Larsen.

SCHOOL CLASS PICTURE
NYKOBING FALSTER

BORNI

BORNI AND ME

BORNI AND ME

NYKOBING F.

BORNI

BORNI

The first girl friend I got to know when I had moved with the Olthaver family to Nykobing Falster was Borni. She was a class mate in the high school class that I had been enrolled in to continue and finish my High school education.

Borni was a tall, slender and pretty girl and I was fairly short . . . . not fat, but a well developed teenager. When I think about it, we probably looked like "Mutt and Jeff", an unfitting pair.

Borni's parents owned a grocery store. I loved to go with Borni to their store and pick up pastry. Once in a while if we had a sleep over at her house, she would run over to the shop and pick up a box with 12 freshly baked Danish pastry and bring them to her house. Unfortunately I loved that pastry and I might eat 7 or 8 of them and she would have the rest.

During that time I obviously was not worried or concerned about my weight. Eating all of that rich and fattening stuff definitely started to put the "calories" in my body.

The trip I took to Cap d'Ail when I was eighteen years old was together with Borni. I think it was actually her idea. It was a good one. We had a grand time. We met some fun and interesting people on the trip and had some long lasting friendships with some of them afterwards.

Borni and I went to several fun parties together. She was usually a bit more reserved than I. That was probably a blessing. That way I wouldn't get too carried away when I was together with Borni. She was a real true friend and I am sorry that I have lost the contact with her.

THE EXOTIC GARDEN

BORNI AND I   VIETNAMESE FRIENDS AND ME

VACATION IN CAP D'AIL

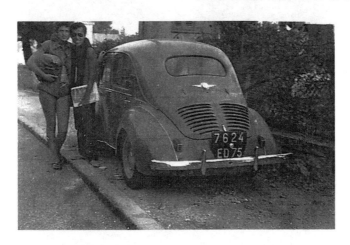

BORNI AND VIETNAM FRIENDS

PERFORMING IN A SAILOR SHOW

PERFORMING IN A VARIETY SHOW

PERFORMING

INGE AND I SQUARE
DANCING

EXERCISING

EXERCISING

JAS-AEROBICS CLASSES

AEROBICS DEMONSTRATION

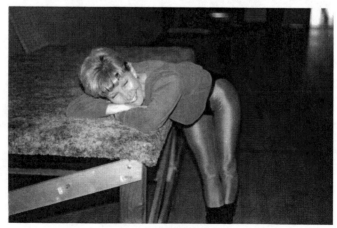

AFTER THE CLASS

FAMILY REUNION AT THE BOESEN HOUSE

FAMILY REUNION AT MIE'S

THE OLTHAVER HOUSE BEFORE AND AFTER

MOVING BACK TO
HASLEV

After I graduated from High School in Nykobing Falster and we moved back to HAslev, I was not sure if I wanted to continue studying, so I started to work at Haslev Apotek, "Pharmacy", where I, for the most part worked in the laboratory filling pills into glasses and containers or I was pouring different medications into glasses.

There was one kind of medication, which I absolutely hated to work with. It was "Torskelevertran", Fish oil. The smell of it would make you feel sick to your stomach. I was later promoted to work at the front desk most of the time. I somehow thought that it was perhaps the beginning to my plans and dreams of continuing in the medical field. Well, evidently it didn't turn out that way.

I was offered a job in the Correspondence Department at SEAS, (Sydostsjaellands Electricitets Actieselskab). It is a great company where both my Dad and brother Arne has worked at various jobs over the years. Arne was still working at SEAS up to his death in January, 1999.

I enjoyed very much working at SEAS. It had a pleasant and relaxing working atmosphere. There were a lot of different departments and I ended up working in three of the different departments.

My first job was typing and being a mail clerk. That was OK, at least I got to see and talk with a lot of the other workers in between sitting in front of a typewriter most of the day. There were a lot of Engineers working at SEAS. After working at the Correspondence Department for 2 years, I moved to the Communications Department, where I was primarily a telephone operator. It was a good job, but not one with any chances of further advancements, so I asked to be moved up to The Technical Department. Here I learned to make technical drawings of transformator stations and drawing maps of the areas and landscapes covered by electricity from SEAS. I particularly enjoyed working in that department as I already liked to paint and draw. I was now working as a draft person.

I worked at SEAS for four years, from August, 1956 to August, 1960. While I was still working there I was trying to keep active and fit even though it was during that time I was suffering from "Anorexia" and my dancing and gymnastics "had taken a back seat".

MODELING
FASHION SHOW

FASHION SHOW

135

MOGENS AND ME

MOGENS AND ME

MOGENS

DANCE RECITAL

COSTUME PARTY

HASLEV

W hile I was still working at SEAS, a girl friend, Erica, suggested one day taking a walk "Around the world". That was a popular hiking and bike trail through the woods. I thought it was a great idea, so we started to make that a daily event. We would either walk or ride our bicycles every morning through the woods before going to work. That was very refreshing, so peaceful and quiet. We would be awake and refreshed, ready to tackle the rest of the day. The walk would take about 45 minutes by doing brisk walking and of course less time when we were riding bikes.

Erica was also my friend, who joined me when we went to "Husassistenternes Fagskole", a Home Economics trade school in Copenhagen, similar to "Courdonbleu" in Paris.

She was actually a beautician, but needed to take some time away from that.

I spent a lot of time at the sports center, where a lot of activity was always taking place. There was usually basketball, tennis or badminton being played.

I started to play badminton with some of my friends. While playing there I met a very handsome young guy, Mogens. We soon became very good friends and we started to date each other. Mogens was studying at the Technical College in Haslev, planning to become an engineer. We spent a lot of time together.

I liked him a lot and when he later moved to Aarhus to attend the Engineering College there I went to visit him for a few days. We became even closer and he started to talk about getting engaged and married. When he had vacation we would go to Fakse Ladeplads, where his parents had a beach house. We could stay there as long as we wanted.

Even though I had a great time together with Mogens, I was not sure that I was quite ready to settle down and get married yet.

I had been dreaming about doing some traveling before tying myself to anybody and I had already decided to go to England and study for a while. I had my heart set on traveling and wanted to see "The World" or at least part of it before making important decisions in regards to marriage and the future.

Needless to say Mogens didn't like my plans, so we broke up.

I often wonder what would have happened and where I would be, if I had married Mogens!?

A VISIT TO
JENSEN'S SHOP

I noticed that some times when my friends and I were playing, sun bathing or just having fun and games in the garden, our neighbors, who had a gift/jewelry shop next door, were often watching us through the fence. They had often invited Sonja and me to come over to see all the new gift items, when they had received a new shipment, I would go over and admire all the beautiful new and exciting things. I knew I could not buy any of it, but that was OK. It was just fun to look at them.

I always thought that Mr. and Mrs. Jensen were such a nice elderly couple. They were very friendly and Mrs. Jensen was a very attractive and graceful lady.

One day Mr. Jensen called across the fence and told me that they had just received a new shipment of costume jewelry and invited me to come over to look at it. I loved to see all the new and shiny items and probably wishing that I could some day own some of it, so I went over to their store to look at all the new shipment.

When I got there he took me to the back room, where all the new items were kept.

Mrs. Jensen wasn't home at that time, but I didn't think anything of it.

I started to look and admire some of all the beautiful jewelry, which was spread out on a large table. I started to comment on some of the things I found prettiest. All of a sudden he started to touch and fumble me. I told him to stop it, but all of a sudden he pushed me down on to the sofa which was right behind me and before I knew it he was right on top of me. He tried to kiss me and attempted to pull my clothes off. I was so scared and started to punch and kick him with all my might. Fortunately, I was a very strong kid, so I managed to kick myself free of him and got out of there.

I ran as fast as I could out of the shop, back to my house, up the stairs and in to my room, sobbing, shaking and still in a state of shock.

I was afraid to tell my family what had happened even though I probably should have. It was a very frightening experience, but I was sure that they would make me feel guilty and tell me that it was probably my own fault. He should have been reported to the police, but never was.

After that day I never looked that way again and avoided their shop as much as I possibly could.

SUMMER CAMP

HASLEV GYMNASIUM

INGE & ME

INGE AND ME AT THE SUMMER CAMP

INGE

INGE

ERICA, HER BROTHER
& FRIENDS

VACATION IN FLENSBORG

ERICA, HER BROTHER
AND ME

VACATIONS

I had taken several small vacation trips through Europe. A couple of trips were to Germany and one was to France and Monaco. I had decided that I would like to see a lot more of Europe and perhaps other parts of the world as well, especially since I wasn't going back to school at this time.

In June, 1956 Borni and I joined a University trip to Cap d'Ail in France. It was right next door to Monte Carlo, Monaco. We enjoyed going there whenever we could. We thought it was so beautiful. We also ventured of to Menton, Nice and Cannes.

We met a lot of young people from other countries. The trip was sponsored by Universitaire Francoise a lot of the young people we met were already studying at the University in Paris. Some of the people we were palling around with most of the time were from Sweden and Norway, but we also got to know some of the students from the Sorbonne or L'Aliance Francoise, who were from many other countries in the world.

Some of the guys and girls we got to know very well were from Viet Nam. We had a lot of fun trying to learn some Viet

Namese. I kept in touch with one of the Viet Nam guys and met him again several years later in Paris.

When we started the trip, which was by train, we boarded the train in Nykobing Falster, We rode through The Netherlands, Belgium and France to Cap d'Ail in the south of France. I still remember how excited we were. When we arrived in Cap d'Ail we were guided to our sleeping quarters. A room with four beds in The Mediterranean Center which we had to share with a couple of Swedish girls, Mai Brit and Britta. They were very sweet and very compatible with Borni and me.

We had some very educational classes, Mostly Historical and geographical. At one of the fun evening functions we had during the vacation, I was crowned as "Miss Cote d'Asure". Of course I felt like "A million bucks". And I was much honored.

I knew for sure that I would want to get down there again some time very soon.

BORNI AND ME IN MONTE CARLO, MONACO

VACATION IN CAP D'AIL

BRITTA AND I

A COUPLE OF SWEDISH FRIENDS

TOURING COTE
D'AZURE

VACATIONS

TOUR GUIDE

ARRIVING AT CAP D'AIL

MONTE CARLO

LEIF AND FRIENDS

TRIP TO HARZEN,
GERMANY WITH LEIF

LEIF AND FRIENDS

VACATIONS

LEIF

BAD HARZBURG

LEIF AND FRIENDS

CHRISTMAS IN DENMARK

I still believe that the way we used to celebrate Christmas in Denmark, especially when I was a kid, is definitely the most special one of all the ones I have experienced in other Countries, Finland, Sweden, France, USA, Hawaii and other places.

If it was snowing and the ground was cowered with snow, it seemed even more exciting and proper.

The pre Christmas time is pretty much the same as everywhere else with lots of preparations, shopping, baking, decorating, letter & Christmas card writing, wrapping, partying etc.

When I was a child I was usually not permitted to help out with any cooking or baking except for Christmas cookies. Therefore it seemed much more fun and special when I could be part of that.

Some time before Christmas our family would usually order ½ pig, which would be dissected and prepared for consumption. Almost every part of it would be used for various meals such as pork, steak, "fleskesteg", ham, pork sausage and other delectable things. Everything was wrapped in special paper, tin foil and containers and placed in the freezer until it was time to consume the different meals.

Christmas Eve, December 24, was always the time for the "Special dinner celebration" with the whole family present. We would always attend church, which was usually at 4:30 or 5 pm in the afternoon. That would give you the best warm feeling that Christmas was actually beginning.

In addition to the usual snacks and nuts, we would often start out with beautifully decorated "Open-face sandwiches" with things like salmon, liver paste, shrimp, smoked eel, pickled herring, roast beef, topped with dill, onion, capers, red pepper etc. to make it even more colorful and appetizing, always served with "Aalborg Aquavit" (snaps) & beer!

Then it was time for "skoaling" and wishing each other "Glaedelig Jul". (Merry Christmas).

Some times we would also have soup as well, but not every time.

The main entre was traditionally either goose or duck served with red cabbage, pickled beets, small sugar browned potatoes, cucumber salad, tomatoes, pickles & home made roles. With that you would have red or white wine.

The dessert was always "Ris a'l'amande" with cherry sauce. It is a rice pudding with crushed almonds, vanilla and whipped cream. One whole almond was placed in the dessert. Whoever found the whole almond would get an almond present. The meal was finally finished off with coffee and cookies.

DANISH CHRISTMAS

"JULEMANDEN",
SANTA CLAUS

When I was still a child I never got to see the Christmas tree until we were finished with the dinner. The tree was placed in the middle of the living room with the doors closed and we were not permitted to go into the room before the doors were finally opened. It was so hard be patient and wait that long, but when you finally got to see the beautifully decorated Christmas tree standing there all lit up it seemed well worth it.

If the presents weren't already placed under the tree, you knew that "Jule manden" (Santa Claus) would soon arrive and deliver the presents. That was always a very exciting moment.

The first few years there would be live candles on the tree but since that could create fires too easily, they were replaced with electric lights.

We started to walk around the tree singing traditional Christmas songs and if Santa was still there he would deal out the presents to everybody. It was such a special evening. Even during the war times there was always plenty of snacks and candy. You often wondered from where it all came? Christmas Day is usually spent either relaxing, enjoying the goodies and presents you had received or you were invited to some family or friends house for dinner.

Second Christmas Day is also a holiday in Denmark and still celebrated with close friends and more big meals and more opportunity to gain even more weight, ... than you really want to!

NATIVITY

HUSASSISTENTERNES FAGSKOLE.

"HUSASSISTENTERNES FAGSKOLE"

HUSASSISTENTERNES
FAGSKOLE

When I started talking about wanting to go to England, my Dad wanted to know what I wanted to do and how I intended to support myself.

I told him that I wanted to attend school and improve my English while watching children as a nanny or as an au'pare. His response to that was simply: "If you want to learn to cook and take care of children? I suggest that you attend a school such as "Husassistendernes Fagskole" in Copenhagen". (Home Economic Trade school).

I did go to "Husassistenternes Fagskole" for 6 months to learn house keeping and child care. It was an excellent and very strict school. Quite frankly, I did learn a lot in that short time. You had to be home every night at 22:00 (10 pm), even on week ends. Next to our school was Engineering College, so we soon managed to have some fun with the guys there through the open windows anyway.

If you wanted the school to help you find a job as a Nanny or House keeper, They were very helpful with that. I thought I would try that for a short while. I started working in a large villa in the outskirts of Copenhagen. The family had three small children, which I was taking care of. They also had a house keeper, as the family entertained a lot. They often had German, English or American guests. I found it interesting and helpful to be able to practice my German and English language skills from time to time. The owner had a piano and organ business and often traveled to other countries to work with other similar business people. Sometimes these people would come for visits or business to Denmark as well.

In the mean time I had been searching for a job in London. When I learned that the Bass family in Highgate, London was in need of a Nanny for their 2 children, I contacted Dr. Bass and told her that I would be able to arrive in May, 1961 and be the Nanny for their two children.

TIMOTHY

LONDON, ENGLAND

LONDON

LONDON

After having enjoyed several vacation trips around Europe, I still had the "travel fever" in my system. I convinced my cousin, Ruth that we should definitely go to England for a while to improve our English, study there and work as nannies or au'pares while attending school in London.

Ruth thought that sounded like a great idea. In the spring of 1961 we flew to London.

I had already made several connections with agencies in London, who were handling the hiring of domestic help, mainly with families who wanted a nanny for their children.

As I mentioned earlier, I worked for a British couple with two small boys. Both the parents were Doctors so it was Dr. and Dr. Bass.

The oldest one of the children was Andrew. He was 6 years old, very intelligent and a little different than most kids his age. The youngest one was Timothy, a sweet little cutie. I just loved those two little fellows.

Andrew was in school part of the day and Timothy was very easy to take care of, I had an easy job.

Their home was a town house situated in a very attractive and rural part of London, called Highgate. I liked the house very much, especially my own room, which was fairly large with a very comfortable double bed. There was a TV set in the room and I had a great view of the City.

You never had the feeling that you were in a large and noisy City. The garden and the surrounding areas were landscaped with a lot of beautiful plants, flowers and attractive trees and bushes. It gave you a nice relaxed feeling once you stepped outside the door, contrary to all the busy hazel and bushel in the City.

Ruth was staying with an elderly couple who lived very close to the family I was staying with in Highgate. They were very friendly. A sweet and charming couple. Mrs. Jones was handicapped and was confined in a wheel chair. Therefore, she needed a lot of care and depended a lot on her husband and Ruth, who was not used to being a caretaker. She was not crazy about having to tend to certain needs of an elderly, sick person, but they were very grateful for her help, and sometimes for my care as well.

I believe he was a retired Physician and they were both delightful.

Syskon College

SOME OF THE STUDENTS FROM THE SCHOOL

At first we started to attend a language school in Piccadilly Circus down town so we had to take "The Tube", (subway) or bus in order to get to the school every day. There of course were a lot of other foreign students. One of them was an Indian boy, Day, whom I got to know very well. I saw him quite often and we later on took a long and very enjoyable trip with several other friends through England and Scotland together.

Later we both changed our studies to another language school, "Syskon College". The school was a lot closer as it was situated in Highgate.

Once again we met and got to know a lot of other foreign students. Some of them were from France, Germany, Iran and India. We often went on sight seeing trips together. One of the German girls, Lillo, became one of our closest friends. She was very outgoing and always ready for fun and excitement, which suited Ruth and me just fine. She introduced us to SOHO, a popular dance restaurant, where young people could get together and dance.

We still kept in touch with some of the people we had met at the Piccadilly Circus school, including Day. He invited Lilo, Ruth and me to join him and some of his friends for a trip through England and up through Scotland. Day had a nice car so he did all the driving.

We drove north along the East Coast of England and stopped for the most part at "B & B's" (Bed and Breakfast Inns). They are usually cheaper than other lodging places and hotels. The breakfast they serve in those places are large enough to carry you through all the day till dinner time, which was our next meal time.

One of the highlights of our trip was Edinburgh Castle, where we got to see the Royal Scottish Tattoo. It was very impressive and one of those things you will always remember.

We saw some very interesting places and towns along the way. The famous Loch Lomond with the Forth Bridge was one of the sights. On the way back to London we drove down the west coast through Lancaster, Warrington, Chester, Stratford-on-Avon and Oxford.

Ruth and I very often went to the Danish Club, which was located close to Highgate. There we would meet other Danish friends and watch movies, shows or other performances.

TRIP TO SCOTLAND

Edinborough Castle

INDIAN FRIENDS   DAY AND ME

RUTH, BILL AND ME

LILO IN LONDON

RUTH AND FRIENDS IN LONDON

LILO

R uth, Lilo and I spent a lot of time together. Sometimes we would go sightseeing or finding new places to "investigate".

One day Lilo, (I think the name is an abbreviation for Liselotte) and I decided to take a trip to Stratford on Avon. The only problem was that we were both "Strapped" for money, so we decided to try "hitch hiking". We were lucky to be picked up by a truck driver who was driving a large "18 Wheeler" truck. We were at first very hesitant, but we jumped into the truck. There was room in the front cabin for both of us. I ended up sitting on top of the hot engine all the way. It was rather unpleasant and my rear end was "toasted" by the time I jumped out of the truck.

The truck driver was very nice and friendly. He talked to us constantly the whole way. I think he was very happy to have company and somebody to talk to.

When I think about us taking that chance, I know of course that it was very stupid and could have been dangerous.

While Ruth and I were in Paris, Lilo also moved there and the three of us were able to get together frequently.

After I moved to USA years later, Lilo came to visit me once or twice. But since that time we have unfortunately lost touch with each other.

LILO IN LONDON

JEANETTE

RUTH AND ME

OXFORD

PARIS

After spending 6 months in London, England, studying English I decided that it was time to learn more languages. I already spoke Danish, Swedish, German and English, which I had learned in High school, the Gymnasium and of course in England. After that you were given the choice to study either French, Spanish, Italian or Latin. I had been studying Latin for a while, as I was planning on getting in to the Medical field later on in my life. I had also been studying a little French, but not enough yet to carry on a conversation, so I decided the best way to learn the language faster and better would be to go to the Country and study there.

Once again I talked Ruth, my cousin in to join me for the trip to Paris, where I already had a connection with a French family and made arrangements to stay with them as their Au'pare and to watch their two sons while attending school. They were a very nice family with their two little boys, Olivier, who was 2 years old and Phillip who was 6 years old and attending school. They were both great kids.

Monsieur & Madame Delicluse was a very attractive couple. They lived in Neu'eis, where they had an apartment on Rue Victor Daix. Neu'eis was a beautiful suburb of Paris in the bois d'Bologne area and close to the river Seine. A lot of the foreign embassies and consulates were situated in that area.

My room, however, was in a different building around the corner. It was on the fourth floor without an elevator and with the toilet (bathroom) which was used by other occupants, situated far from my room . . . . It was far from "luxury".

I soon found out that I had to get some kind of container to use during the night instead of having an unpleasant and maybe embarrassing trip to the toilet. I sure didn't want to meet anybody else on that trip.

The room was very small and narrow with a French balcony facing out to the back yard. I had just enough room for the bed and a small desk and closet. It was a far cry from my own room in Denmark and the room I had while in London. But after seeing some of the rooms other student or friends were offered to stay in in Paris it were not too bad.

Both Monsieur and Madame Delicluse had been living and working in the USA for a couple of years, so they spoke excellent English. When he wanted to tell a funny joke or something interesting to me he always changed the language from French to English, as he knew that I would understand it better. As far as helping me to learn the French language faster, they were no help.

PARIS

PHILLIP

OLIVER

MADAMA DELICLUSE
WITH PHILLIP

PARIS

MORE PARIS

Ruth was staying with a family in a different part of the city. When we wanted to get together we decided to meet either at the school, L'Aliance Françoise, or at some central part of the city.

Our German friend, Lilo, that we got to know while we were in England, also followed us to Paris. The three of us once again were able to get together from time to time. We saw each other every day usually at the school or sight seeing. We loved to tour around and look at some of all the beautiful monuments, la Tour Eiffel (The Eiffel Tower), Basilique du Sacre-Coeur, (The sacred Heart Cathedral), L'Arc de Triomphe (The Triumph Arch) and La Louvre, just to mention a few. There are a lot of beautiful sights in Paris. Some times we would also get together in the evening, either to see a movie or to some function we had been invited to.

As much as I enjoyed living in Paris, I will have to admit that I was more contend living in London. My cousin, Ruth, Lilo and other friends as well as the school, was close by and easier to get to in London.

Once the Parisians heard that you had a foreign accent they could be rather unfriendly and ignorant . . . at least at that time. You definitely got the impression that they did not like foreigners and that could be very unpleasant. I have since been back to Paris several times and I noticed that people's attitude had changed considerably. However the people living in the country side were quite different and usually very nice.

One of the first days we met each other down town to get registered at the language school, L'Aliance Francoise as we had to attend that school to learn and improve our French before we would be able to start at the Sorbonne. I definitely wanted to continue there and eventually get my master degree in language art.

My plans were still either to become an international correspondent, getting in to the Medical field or become a Stewardess. At that time you had to be able to speak several languages to work and travel internationally and I still wanted to "Travel the World".

I still had not given up on my first plans of becoming a dancer, which I actually did later. I taught Gymnastic, Ballet, Jas-aerobics and Physical fitness for several years.

One of the Vietnamese guys I met while I was vacationing in Cap d'Ail, was still living in Paris and studying at the Sorbonne. We would get together for dinner and parties from time to time. He usually invited me to some of the functions going on at the school. I also got to know a very famous Spanish artist by the name: Federico Aguilar y Alquaf, who actually lived in Barcelona, Spain. I was later informed that Frederico had been in a severe car accident and I never heard any more from him after that.

I will have to confess that I have since lost the connection with most of the people I met and knew during my youth but I often think that it could be fun and interesting to see them all again and find out, what has happened to them, what they have been doing, and where in the world they might be.

PARIS

NGUYEN

FREDERICO

THE INVITATION TO USA

While living and studying in Paris I suddenly received a phone call from a Danish friend, Jorgen Sander Larsen. He was a friend of the Olthaver family in Denmark.

I went to Haslev Gymnasium in the same grade as his sister Ellen Birthe and my "step" sister Bente went to school together with Jorgen. He was now a NATO Commander stationed in Norfolk, Virginia, USA and was at the moment on a business trip to Paris and other places in Europe.

I was very surprised to hear from him, as I had not seen or talked to him in a very long time and quite frankly did not know that he was now stationed in the USA. Jorgen was married and had two young sons and was at the time living in Virginia Beach, Virginia.

"How are you doing and how do you like living in Paris?" he asked. I told him that I loved living there and that I was going to continue studying at the Sorbonne. He continued, "Well, how would you like to go to USA?" Shockingly I replied, "No, are you crazy? I can't do that. I have to stay here and study". He insisted: "Just listen to me! It can be very easy and simple, ... all you have to do is just go to the American Embassy here in Paris, bring your passport and they will stamp a NATO Visa right in your passport. You can go home to Denmark for a week or two and then . . . . off you go". We argued back and forth for a while as I wasn't going to give in to him and ruin my study plans. I also knew that my family would not like that idea either.

Jorgen added that he was going to make all my travel arrangements. I could stay with him and his family in Virginia Beach, help take care of the kids and go to school at the same time, if I wanted to. He didn't tell me much about the arrangements at the time, but he had it all figured out.

I had to admit that it sounded way too easy to believe, but was, at the same time, very tempting. Maybe I could continue the studying later on.

It was now February, 1962.

After being home in Denmark for almost two weeks visiting my family and friends, I was to board a Danish Freight ship in Copenhagen according to the arraignments that Jorgen was taking care of.

Jorgen was a very clever man and a bit of a "Wheeler-dealer", so the plans were that I was to escort/transport a large shipment of "Royal Copenhagen China" to USA, . . . unbeknown to me. It was an order that some Commanding Admiral had ordered and had to have it sent to USA, "The inexpensive way". I was the "Guinea pig".

THE BOAT TRIP ON M.S. URUGUAY TO USA.

RELAXING ON THE SHIP M.S. URGUAY

ARRIVING IN NEW YORK

ARRIVING IN NY, USA.

ON BOARD THE SHIP

I thought I was going to fly 1st. Class . . . . well, maybe, but I admit, even though it was a fairly small ship, "Uruguay", and it only carried about 25 passengers it was a fun filled and enjoyable trip with a group of very nice and fun loving people. The sail trip lasted two weeks, so we sometimes had to come up with our own card games, plays and other forms of entertainment for amusement. The ship had a very nice dining room, a bar and a game room. I thought it was interesting that we all dressed up every day before we went up for dinner. The food on board was excellent, maybe even better than what you sometimes get on an expensive luxury liner.

I do remember being sea sick for a couple of days. We were hitting some stormy weather while we were getting close to Iceland and the seas were getting pretty rough. Once I recovered from that I was good for the rest of the trip.

We finally arrived in New York after two weeks sailing. The first thing you see, of course is, The Statue of Liberty when you enter New York harbor. That is a very impressive sight.

THE ARRIVAL IN NEW YORK

When the ship finally arrived in New York harbor in March, 1962 the Sander Larsen Family was there to meet me.

After welcoming me to USA and helping me through The Customs, we went to eat at a restaurant and then started driving south to get to their home in "Thoroughgood" Village, Virginia Beach.

Of course they had a lot of questions to ask me about the sail trip, how the family in Denmark was doing, as well as what I had been doing up to this point.

It was a long ride from New York to Virginia Beach. When we finally arrived at the house, it was very late and we were all pretty tired.

I was given the impression that I was just going to watch the kids. They had two boys, Peter, who was nine years old and Lars, who was five years old, but as it turned out, Tove, Jorgen's wife had other plans. She expected me to do a lot more than "Baby sitting", like cleaning the house, some cooking and washing their clothes as well. On top of that she could be very demanding and unreasonable. She seemed to be more interested in all the luncheons, cocktail parties and other functions she attended.

My plans about going to school "went down the drain"!.

After a couple of months I called my Danish Dad, (Anton). I told him that I was NOT very happy there. I wanted to return back home to Denmark. "Please send me some money, I am not happy here".

He sent the money for my flight ticket and I was going to make the arrangements for the flight home.

In the mean time I started getting to know some young people my own age and started to "date".

The Sander Larsen's socialized a lot since he was a senior Navy officer and NATO Commander, therefore they also entertained often as well. Consequently Tove was becoming more and more demanding of me and they were just paying me "Pocket money".

The guy, Jaque, who I was dating was a Navy Lieutenant, but shortly after our first few dates he told me that he had been planning to get out of the Navy, go back to college in Michigan and wanted to become a journalist. Before he left to go to Michigan he asked his house mate, Phil, a US Marine Officer to take care of me while he was gone.

Phil decided to take that offer seriously, so as soon as he could, he started to call me and inviting me out.

TOVE S. LARSEN, A FRIEND AND I READY
FOR A LUNCHEON

I declined the offer . . . . at first, but then decided that it was probably OK to see him once anyway. That meeting turned out to be more than "one date". Jacque called several times at the Larsen house, but was usually informed that I was at Phil's house. One day when he called the beach house (Phil's house), he told us that he was planning to come down to Virginia Beach for a visit in October. Phil told him: "Why don't you wait till November and come down for the wedding on November second?" "What wedding?" was the reply. "Jeanette and I are getting married" Phil responded.

I don't think anything was said after that, ... and unfortunately we never heard from Jacque again.

The wedding for Phil and me took place November 2, 1962.

We are still married fifty years later after many Military separations and we celebrated our Golden Anniversary on a River Cruise November 2, 2012. Before we left on the cruise our daughter, Annette, son Tony and daughter in law Veronica had a lovely Anniversary Party for us at their Club House in La Jolla, California.

I have enjoyed a great life in The United States and was blessed with three beloved children and two Grandsons. We had to move many times during my husband's Military Career and finally retired and settled in San Diego, California.

During all that time I have never lost contact with my family in Finland, Sweden and Denmark. We have made many trips back home to Scandinavia and many family members have visited with us in The United States. The last trip to Scandinavia took place in 2011.

PHIL AND JEANETTE READY FOR THE MC BALL

THE SCANDINAVIAN
TRIP IN 2011

I n 2011 I decided to take a trip to Scandinavia. It had been several years since I had visited or seen any of my family. Besides something was telling me that I had to go and see my sisters, especially Sylvia, who was now the oldest and only one of my siblings still, living in Finland.

My husband didn't want to go with me this time, so I brought a niece, Eila, (My brother, Leo's daughter), who is living in Alabama. She also wanted to see the family in Finland after several years.

I called my sister Sylvia to let her know that our niece, Eila and I were planning to come to Finland for a visit in May-June, 2011.

Sylvia wasn't home, so I called her daughter, "Tuta", to find out that her Mother was very ill with cancer and lying in the hospital.

Right away I knew that I definitely wanted to go and see my sister and make the trip as soon as possible. Of course I wanted to see all the rest of the families as well.

I started my flight in San Diego, California and met Eila in Chicago to join me for the rest of the trip to Helsinki, Finland. We wanted to go there first, mainly to see Sylvia and the family there before continuing the rest of the trip through Sweden and Denmark.

We also wanted to visit a couple of cousins, Ralf and Rainer and their families, who live in the south western part of Finland, near the Island Hitis, where my Mom is from.

We went to visit Sylvia at the hospital every day while we were in Helsinki. She didn't look too bad at that time, but it was obvious that she had lost a lot of weight. We could tell she was very happy to see both of us.

After staying in Helsinki, Dragsfjerd and Hitis we wanted to go to Umeaa, Sweden to visit my other sister, whose name also happen to be Eila.

We stayed with her for about one week. It was great to see her as well and I wish we could have spent some more time with her.

Our original plans were to travel down through Sweden either by train or bus to maybe do some sight seeing and stop a couple of places along the way, but since we knew that we had to cover a lot of territory, visit a lot of family and friends and we only had one month for the whole trip, we decided that we had better fly directly to Copenhagen, which we did.

My Danish Niece, Mie greeted us at the Airport. We stayed at her house most of the time we were in Denmark. She has also been visiting me several times in the USA including Hawaii.

SUOMILAISLAPSET TANSKASSE YHDISTYS.
(Formed in 1992).
(Finnish Children in Denmark)

SUOMALAISLAPSET TANSKASSA YHDISTYS YEARLY MEETING IN SEPTEMBER, 1997.
Finnebørnsmøde på Sjælland

Så er vi der atter - Auri og Erkki - for vi synes, at det er på tide, at vi ses igen.

Vi har oven i købet en virkelig god anledning, nemlig at vores "amerikanske finnebarn" - Jeanette Shaw fra USA er i Danmark og selvfølgelig gerne vil møde ligesindede, og vi vil jo alle sammen også gerne møde Jeanette.

Vi ser derfor gerne stor tilslutning til vores efterårsmøde og opfordrer Jer til at komme og bidrage til og nyde nogle gode timer sammen.

Vi beder Jer alle sammen om at møde op mellem kl. 12.00 og 13.00

L Ø R D A G den 27 september

Sted: **Sct. Georgsgilaet**
          Møllevej 6 A
          4180 Sorø

Traktementet består af Buffet: Frikadeller, kold glaceret skinke, udskåre culottesteg, kartoffelsalat og mixed salat samt tærte med créme fraiche.
Derefter kaffe med småkager.

Pris pro persona inkl. leje af lokale, porto m.m. er ca. kr. 100,- .
Jo flere vi bliver - jo billigere bliver det.

Der kan købes rødvin, hvidvin og/el. øl/vand.

Telefonisk tilmelding inden den 24 september til:

Auri Henriksen	*eller*	***Erkki Trige***
53 63 20 63		53 57 45 51

Mange venlige hilsener
og på gensyn

ONE OF THE FINISH-DANISH MEETINGS

While we were in Denmark, of course we visited the Danish family I had stayed with during the war and some childhood friends, including Inge and Poul. (Inge was my first class mate in Haslev Elementary School. Poul was also a class mate, but not till we started attending "Haslev Gymnasium", where he was a College Student).

Unfortunately both Arne and Bente, (My Danish brother and sister), has passed away, but their children, (my nephews and Nieces) are all still living in Denmark and in a way I have always been feeling closer to them both in age and other wise. My husband calls Mie and myself "Sisters" as we are fairly close in age . . . and spirit.

Arne's son, Anker and his wife Susie and daughter are still living in the same house, where I used to live and grew up. Needless to say we visited them as well.

Bente's sons, Finn, Torben and Alex all live in the Copenhagen area and while we were there Torben and wife Carin had invited the whole family together for a very nice family reunion.

One other thing I definitely also wanted to do in Denmark was partake in the Finish-Danish yearly meeting of the organization "SUOMILAISLAPSET TANSKASSA YHDISTYS", (Finnish children in Denmark), which I still belong to.

The organization was formed by the Finish children, who were sent to Denmark during the war and who for the most part are still living in Denmark.

One of my Finish friends, Rut Gronroos, who is also a member of the organization got me involved by paying my first tuition, since I was now living in USA.

In order to catch the flight back to USA we had to return to Helsinki one more time. That gave me an opportunity to see my sister Sylvia again.

I feel very blessed to be able to say "god buy" to her at that time, as she passed away a couple of days after wards.

THE CHALLENGE

To me this has been a major project to write this book, but thanks to a lot of friends and my family it actually has come to a reality. Some memories has been buried deep down in my mind and had to be "pulled out" little by little. Just trying to find some of the right pictures for the book have been a challenge. Some of them were in photo albums and a lot of them I had to find in boxes in the addict or in the garage. (I am not as organized as I used to be.)

A Finish-Danish friend, Kai Palomaki Schmidt, a retired school principle has also written a book about his happy childhood in Denmark after being sent there during the Finish-Russian war as a seven (7) years old boy in 1942. He was very lucky, like most of us Finish kids, to be sent to a good family. Kai is the foreman for the Finish-Danish organization "SUONALAISLAPSET TANSKASSA YHDISTYS", which I still belong to. I know that Kai feel very fortunate and blessed to be sent to a home where they took very good care of him, treated him just like one of their own children and gave him a good education.

CPSIA information can be obtained at www.ICGtesting.com
Printed in the USA
LVOW11s2156310515

440658LV00001B/76/P